THE NEED
TO SAY "NO"

How to Be Bullish and Not Bullied

THE NEED
TO SAY "NO"

THE IMPORTANCE OF
SETTING BOUNDARIES IN
LOVE, LIFE & YOUR WORLD

JILL BROOKE

⟫⟫ hatherleigh

》》 hatherleigh

Hatherleigh Press is committed to preserving and protecting the natural resources of the earth. Environmentally responsible and sustainable practices are embraced within the company's mission statement.

Visit us at www.hatherleighpress.com and register online for free offers, discounts, special events, and more.

The Need to Say "No"
Text copyright © 2013 Jill Brooke

Library of Congress Cataloging-in-Publication Data is available upon request.
ISBN: 978-1-57826-461-2

Cover and Interior Design by Carolyn Kasper and Dede Cummings / DCDESIGN

Printed in the United States
10 9 8 7 6 5 4 3 2 1

ACKNOWLEDGMENTS

I would like to thank Stephen Gerringer, one of the guiding lights leading the Joseph Campbell Foundation, for taking me down a rabbit hole to discover ancient bull myths and symbols. He not only provided access to resources found in Joseph Campbell's personal library—preserved and maintained by the OPUS Archives and Research Center—but always brought smiles with his missives, which were signed, "Metaphorically Yours, Stephen."

I am also grateful to my sister-in-law Denise Brooke who, when cleaning out a closet, stumbled on Dr. Henry Cloud's 1992 book *Boundaries: When to Say Yes, When to Say No to Take Control of Your Life* when I was about to turn in this project. Dr. Henry Cloud is someone whom I respect and admire for his knowledge of both the spiritual and the practical. He has both strength and sensitivity, as well as the most practical advice for anyone needing boundaries.

Thank you also to Susan Rivers at Yale University's Center for Emotional Intelligence for giving me both research and her time. Also, a special thanks to those who truly love and study bulls and cattle, including researcher Christine Barley and bull rider and teacher Gary Leffew.

Kerry Kennedy is not only a friend but also a role model in saying no to adult bullies. As she said at a speech for the RFK Center for Justice and Human Rights, "Moral courage isn't standing up just to governments and armies, but friends and families. It is the willingness to be ostracized by your community for what you believe is right." I thank you for letting me use excerpts from that speech in this book.

I would also like to acknowledge David Simon. No one has taught me more about digging deep into emotion to unearth those nuggets of truth that throb in all of us. He is my writing partner and pal, and I am so grateful to access his big brain and heart, which he gives of so generously. He is the wisest of bulls.

Last but not least, I want to thank my editor Anna Krusinski for her grace and talent, and for never minding when I called to ask, "What do you think of this?" And the bulls in my life who offered expertise and encouragement for this project, including Fern Siegel, Carolyn Tenney, Andrea Kates, Roger Friedman, Leslie Lampert, Robert Albertson, Elena Castaneda, Suzanne Murphy, and Nancy Behrman. And my husband, Gary, who over the years has revealed himself to be the strongest of bulls.

CONTENTS

INTRODUCTION

In the bullpen of life, there are many bulls you have to deal with—including yourself. After all, there are over 800 breeds, each with distinctive personality traits.

Some bulls you meet are cold-blooded, while others respond to warmth. Some are bred to be combative, while others make friends with fellow animals and herd the group to safe havens and prosperity. And yes, of course there are those stubborn types that when triggered can be bullheaded. But many also have the capacity for tenderness and tenacity.

Too often, we look in fear and awe at a bull's physical strength and don't examine its hidden complexities and potential for offering so much wisdom. Because bulls, like humans, can be misunderstood creatures.

For example, in bullfights, a bull doesn't flare its nostrils, stomp its feet, and charge into attack simply upon seeing the color red.

In fact, bulls are color blind. However, bulls are very sensitive to movement, and it's the waving of the matador's cape that activates a gladiatorial response. Did you know that a fighting bull is never used in the ring twice? Bulls learn from their mistakes. This is why the finesse you use to move towards a bull, as well as to steer it away, will determine your success in joining any herd; whether it's at home, at work, or in your community.

"Everything that irritates us about others can lead us to a better understanding of ourselves."

—CARL JUNG

We all have a part of the bull in us, but we access different parts of its character. For those of us with kinder, gentler temperaments, it can feel as though the world is full of stampeding bulls that are selfish and exploitive, often turning into workplace bullies, or adult versions of those you endured in school. With this book, you will learn to build an invincible shield to protect you from those who seek to overwhelm, intimidate, and take advantage of your good nature. You know them: The brother who tells you that you will be taking care of doddering Dad, "Because you're better at it;" the sister who guilts you into bailing her out financially; the boss who dismisses your concerns; the soccer coach or school mom who snubs you; the teenager who screams because he knows you'll cave in; or the friends who request a million favors and then vanish the second you need help.

Somehow, some way, those human bulls are different animals than we are. But they are worth studying because, while bulldozing through life, they often achieve success. They rise to the top of their professions and social circles while you are left choking on the dust left behind, shaking your head, and lamenting why life isn't fairer.

Many of us find ourselves in this situation because we have been burdened by the desire to please. It gives us joy to help and serve. It feels good to be needed. We are taught that saying no is rude and selfish, and we should say no only to drugs and strangers. Furthermore, if you have a big heart and generosity of spirit, you shouldn't expect the same type of reciprocity. Why? Because you are supposed to lead by example.

Like you, I enjoy being a giver. But sometimes a feeling of discomfort stirred in the pit of my stomach, and I intuitively felt there was an imbalance that needed to be corrected.

One day I was in a class where a teacher advised that, although it is counterintuitive to what you have been taught, you must create clear boundaries or your life container can be drained of its vital juices. However, if protected, it can turn into a force as strong as a bull.

With the help of this bull, you can activate the wisdom of your warrior spirit and become far more effective in getting what you want in life while maintaining your values as a decent, honorable person.

The Need to Say "No" will guide you to gain command of your relationships by creating boundaries and zones of self-respect.

Plus, by learning to say no, you won't be so overstretched and may find time for all those activities languishing on your to-do list. You'll be less exhausted and stressed, and can perform more optimally. By saying no, you will have more time to make a real difference to the causes you care about and the people you truly love. In fact, you could actually become more bullish about life. Wouldn't that be nice?

How do we become successful bulls, learning to get what we want without feeling bullied, bamboozled, or bulldozed by those around us? The keys to opening this door are already in your possession. The wisdom of the bull is waiting for you.

PART I

BULL WISDOM THROUGHOUT HISTORY

At the age of three, Carl Jung, the founder of analytical psychology, began having dreams featuring an old man with white hair and the horns of a bull. This spirit guide called himself Philemon. He would become the Swiss psychiatrist's lifelong friend. Jung credited Philemon for helping him to develop the concepts of the extroverted and introverted personalities, as well as the theory of the collective unconscious. Philemon informed Jung that in our unconscious lie layers of wisdom accumulated over time. As Jung wrote in his private diaries (which scholars weren't allowed to access until 2009), there are things in our minds that we may not produce which have their own existence. It is not only a collective unconscious but a life force of superior insight that we can all access if we open our eyes and our hearts.

Jung was one of many great men and women who forged an alliance with the bull spirit. Buddha was another.

In Chinese history, there is a group of sacred paintings known as *The Ten Bulls*

THE NEED TO SAY "NO"

of Zen. Each illustration is accompanied by a poem or short piece of descriptive prose describing the quest of a student in pursuit of a bull. In Buddhism, the bull is a metaphor for enlightenment and self-discovery; therefore, it is the student's quest to find the bull and tame it. In the first painting, the bull is lost and its owner is trying to locate it. Determined to continue his quest, the student finds footprints on the riverbank. Upon seeing the bull, the student engages in an epic battle requiring focus, discipline, and strategy. Finally, the student learns to kNOw himself. Yes, the word *no* is threaded into the word *knowledge* for a reason! He brings the bull under control by recognizing the animal in himself and says no to its baser destructive instincts, instead using the strength of reason and wisdom to live in harmony with all beings.

Guess it's not a surprise that Buddha's birthday occurred during the month of Taurus—the sign of the bull. Or that in Nordic

mythology, Thor was aligned with the bull
when not throwing all those thunderbolts.

How many times have you looked up to the
sky wishing for more? Have you noticed the
constellation of Taurus? It is no coincidence
that Taurus, the first constellation in the
Jewish zodiac, and *aleph*, the first letter in
the Hebrew alphabet, both resemble a bull.

Ancient legend has it that the bull was
born from the union of the sun and the moon,
making it a rare androgynous creature
with both male and female characteristics,
a yin and yang of cosmic balance. Because
the head and the horns of the bull strongly
resemble female reproductive organs, the
great goddesses throughout the ages have
taken the bull as their friend and advisor.
Egypt's Hathor, the protector of women and
goddess of joy, prevailed and said no to the
practice of any animal sacrifice of the bull.

Therefore, while the bull's male strength
and versatility were able to provide spiritual advice on careers, resourcefulness, and

managing power, with these female connections the bull could also offer help with
fertility and domestic life. In fact, a respect
and love of bulls was a belief both men and
women could embrace throughout the ages.

Bull cults still survive today. Current
adaptations include bull riding, where cow-
boys must stay on a bucking bull for eight
seconds. This wildly popular sport continues
to build in popularity throughout the United
States, and there are now both national and
international bull riding events. And, of
course, there is the spectacle of bullfighting
in Spain, Portugal, France, and many South
American countries. But the bullfights taking
place around us every day in playgrounds,
schools, bedrooms, and boardrooms are
equally dangerous, and require skill to manage effectively. With the following strategies,
you will gain the secret knowledge to steer
all the human bulls in your life where you
want them without waving a white flag.

Olé.

PART II

FINDING YOUR INNER BULL

Before we corral the bulls around us and learn to manage them, we first have to examine what type of bull we are.

This is a time for honesty. No BS (a.k.a. bullshit). Do you know where that phrase comes from?

Some etymologists believe its origins could be from the 17th-century when *bull* meant nonsense, or from the French word *boul,* which means "deceit." But the answer may be derived by once again looking to the bull for helpful insight.

Cattle have four stomachs and a built-in fermenting system for processing an astonishing range of material—grass, grain, corn—as well as truths, half-truths, delusions, and family myths. Cattle chew for hours at a time to squeeze out every possible nutrient no matter how small. Yes, just like a human bull will take a nugget of information and stretch it like salt water taffy to dazzle a date with inflated bravado, or impress a boss with puffed up credentials, cattle can effortlessly take grainy grub and transform it into a five-star, protein-rich dish. But what comes out in the end is still a lot of waste. In fact, it can be toxic and contribute to global warming and the cooling of common sense and empathy.

If we are truthful, BS is a temporary solution that takes the sting out of our feelings of inadequacy. We are all frantically trying to be relevant and upbeat because forces are working against us to make us irrelevant: high-tech machinery, the Internet, our birthdays, the widening gap of educated adults who can't find decent-paying jobs, a justice system that feels broken, the dizzying pace of everyday life. If you feel like you are failing to achieve all you expected, what better solution than to paint a happier picture for yourself? We want fairy tales because reality has become so hard, and real change requires too much effort and sacrifice. BS is different than a lie because it is based on exaggeration or hope. Someone who lies knows they are lying and has a sadistic disregard for truth.

BS in the good old days was an art. And now it's a disease. It's a pervasive illness that is accepted as everyday behavior until we are healed from the belief that who we are can never be enough. It is a stumbling block to reaching emotional and financial solvency. We all have contributed to our share of BS. But it shouldn't be with ourselves.

By fortifying our confidence, smarts, and skills, we can say no to BS and be part of the growing herd who listens to the calling of the bull whisperers. By being bullish about substance, we not only earn respect but also respect ourselves.

BREEDING

Bulls are extremely curious creatures—a kind of Sherlock Horns. They investigate everything. If you are having a problem with your boss, spouse, or friend, look to your past. Human bulls who don't question the source of their beliefs can fall prey to controlling people and repeating mistakes. As with most things in life, it starts with your family.

If Mama or Papa Bull never let you disagree, you may believe setting boundaries creates abandonment. It doesn't. If they were rigid and controlling, you may dodge confrontation and not have learned to discuss differences confidently. You little bulls who lived with alcoholic or abusive parents understandably will seek peace at all costs, often denying your own needs. Because if you don't give yourself permission to say no, you are learning to say yes to bad things, which can create abusive or unsatisfying relationships.

It can also sidetrack you into agreeing to do projects or tasks that undermine your ability to excel at your work and life. Human bulls need practice in saying no and this can start at any age.

SEEING IS BELIEVING

Bulls have almost total panoramic vision. They are acutely aware of all animals around them. They know precisely where danger and opportunity lurk. You have to see a problem before it can be fixed. That is the equivalent of striking a bull's-eye, a term derived from the 1830s, when the target of English archers was the white skull of a bull and hitting its eye was the ultimate accomplishment.

But to hit the target—in this instance, setting better boundaries—we must have solid aim. And that means overcoming obstacles with single-minded focus.

For example, part of the reason that human bulls find it difficult to say no is because they have unfulfilled developmental needs. Do you still yearn for a caring father and spend a lifetime pleasing others to feel worthy? Your mother may have thought your brother was smarter, and to this day, you still doubt your own intelligence. You may regret you didn't get a better education. Until you grieve for what you did not have and let go of desired expectations, you cannot focus on what you can have.

WE ARE CREATURES OF HABIT, BUT HABITS CAN CHANGE

A switch goes on and the mechanical bull automatically twists and turns. Unlike other members of the animal kingdom, human bulls have a different kind of switch. Your inner "Urban Cowboy" provides you with the ability to analyze your urges and think long-term.

Learning requires energy and focus. Re-learning and un-learning require even more and the stubborn part of the bull inside you will put up one hell of a fight. Knowing that habits have been formed over the years, don't be surprised that it requires concerted effort to loosen its grip on your neck.

Much of human behavior occurs without decision making or conscious thought. To change behavior, you need to become aware of your vulnerabilities and develop strategies to counteract them.

Start practicing on small targets. At restaurants or when choosing a movie, practice saying, "No thank you, I would prefer . . . ." If you're in a train car with passengers speaking at ear-splitting levels, don't accept discomfort. Move to another seat.

Find ways to stay away from people or situations that diminish your resolve to say no. It could be temporarily avoiding walking down a hall where there's a candy machine or where some co-workers congregate. Or, when with people who make you feel uncomfortable, develop an action such as pressing two fingers together or standing up taller to trigger confidence. Another strategy is to identify an emotional experience you are feeling and then label the emotion using words such as peeved, pressured, insecure, angry, feeling left out, misunderstood, or overworked. A lightbulb should then go on to remind you how to act with each situation. You can manage and control your behavior by slowing down, regrouping, breathing to stay calm, and thinking about trying the plan. With practice, it becomes more natural until one day it becomes habit.

BUILDING FENCES

Bulls mostly live in open fields surrounded by fences. These boundaries are erected for protection. The bulls know exactly where their space begins and ends, and become defensive if their territory is invaded. Human bulls need to build boundaries for their own security; otherwise, they get trampled on.

These internal boundaries are like property deeds. You have ownership over your life and must define what is yours and what belongs to neighbors and friends. You must establish what your responsibilities are to others and for yourself. Building strong fences gives you freedom and power. Unlike concrete walls, the fences where most bulls live have openings, including a gate. This means that they are not shut out from fresh air and the outside world. It also means that whatever stinks from inside can exit. We need to keep things that will nourish us inside our fences and keep things that harm us outside. As the great cosmic bull knows, a gateway to learning must always be open.

PART III

THE BULLS IN
THE BULLPEN

Everyone wants a bull market where they work. A bull market means prosperity, success, and a prolonged period of abundance. The terms *bull market* and *bear market* are derived from the animals themselves. Bears are lethargic and bulls are spirited. When bulls attack, they will thrust their horns up in the air, while bears will swipe their paws down. Therefore, a bull is symbolic of an up market.

In any office, there will be aggressive bulls who want to dominate. Because of fierce competition, it will bring out the worst in them. These include the shouting bosses, the duplicitous colleagues who take credit for ideas, or the co-worker who asks you to do tasks outside your job description. What do you do when you feel unappreciated and undermined in the workplace?

Activate your inner bull and learn from successful bulls. Like any group of people categorized for better understanding, human bulls can be divided into groups. Each of them has distinct characteristics that help us

THE NEED TO SAY "NO"

not only to recognize their behavior, but also gives us the chance to communicate more effectively. It always helps to know whom you are dealing with, and how to make the best of your situation.

What follows is a map for you to start your hero's journey as you confront the ten types of bulls around you.

TEN TYPES OF BULLS IN THE WORKPLACE

TEDDY BEAR BULL

The Teddy Bear Bull summons the bull spirit of the 26th president of the United States, Teddy Roosevelt. He cared deeply about fairness, justice, women's rights, and the average guy getting a "square deal." He was determined to combat corporate cronyism. But when you're in a ring with the powerful bulls of big business who want to destroy your progressive policies, you cannot rely solely on personality and brute strength.

Considered one of the best-read presidents, Roosevelt combed the fine print, not just the headlines. He loved debating with the best minds and didn't use his opponents as props for fixed fights. Roosevelt liked chewing on ideas—not just his, but others as well. He created what is known as the bully pulpit, a safe place for opposing viewpoints to be discussed, so the best ideas surface and flourish. In essence, he was the namesake of the popular TED conferences, which feature speakers with ideas worth spreading, as well as of the cuddly "Teddy" bear, a moniker earned after he refused to kill a trapped animal because he deemed it unsportsmanlike.

You want to be a Teddy Bear Bull. He doesn't accept the status quo and isn't afraid to say no. He will also make Herculean efforts to get results by using his knowledge and his strength of character.

BULL-ET POINT JOHN

Not everyone is a swashbuckling hero like Teddy Bear Bull. But anyone can be a Bull-et Point John or Jane. They are also the kind of person that the Teddy Bear Bull wants on his team. They use research and bullet points to analyze business plans and find opportunities. Other bulls will try to overwhelm them with reams of unsubstantiated research and even resort to screaming. Bull-et Point John and Jane stay calm, probe deeper, and then ask, "How do you know those studies aren't BS? Who paid for the study, how many people were sampled, what other surveys are focused on this topic? Perhaps the researchers were out to prove their own thesis." Bull-et Point John and Jane are bullish on substance and consider President John Adams a hero. Adams lost a case early in his career on a technicality. At first, he blamed his law partner. Then he realized that one must search for treasures with their own fingers. Bull-et

Point John and Jane sift the truth from BS to achieve success.

THE BRAD PITT BULL AND SANDY BULL-OCK

With dashing looks and seductive smiles, the Sandy Bull-ock and Brad Pitt Bull say no in the most charming way. When the boss presents an idea, they smile, nod their head in agreement, and then point out a better way to achieve the company goal, while giving the boss credit with a wink. Working on a team project, Sandy Bull-ock's soothing voice makes all bulls gravitate toward her as she cheers on colleagues for every idea. Even when Sandy or Brad Pitt Bulls say no, they never raise their voice. You won't hear them bellow that someone is an idiot for having a crazy idea. They visibly contemplate suggestions before coming to a conclusion, and then make a concerted effort to explain why they have decided to nix the idea. This, of course, encourages you to try to please them both and come up with a better idea next time. Always informed about current trends, Sandy Bullock and Brad Pitt Bulls never slip off the pop culture food chain.

Sitting Bull

In our culture, yes is perceived as moving forward or rushing to an opportunity, while no is considered a stumbling block, a big blaring stop sign to progress. In actuality, saying no doesn't always stop movement. In fact, when looked at in a fresh way, saying no can be like pressing a pause button to consider alternate routes that can offer a better and more enriching outcome.

Which is why there are times to learn from the Sitting Bull.

The Sitting Bull knows you can be effective by sitting and waiting before asserting your ideas. He has trained himself to fight the impulse to butt in with opinions until he can accurately assess their merits and flaws.

He is not the proverbial China Shop Bull. In fact, Sitting Bull, the Native American chief who led the Sioux tribe to victories against unfair United States government's expansion policies, was in the minority, outnumbered by his opponents. But he knew precisely when to seize an opportunity and use it to his advantage. He didn't mind waiting until the perfect time. While waiting, the Sitting Bull amasses information to effectively negotiate with co-workers, bosses, clients, friends, and relatives. In Sitting Bull's view, you are defined by two traits: your patience when you have nothing and your attitude when you have everything. He is wise and adaptable.

STANDING BULL

If you have a great product, believe in it. Trust your primal bull instinct. Stand tall. A very famous human bull was a struggling writer who wrote a script that Hollywood loved. The big Hollywood executives patted him on the head and offered him trinkets to go away. He stood strong because he wanted to act in the film as well as getting the writing credit. He did not budge. They offered him more trinkets that jingled like gold. He was tempted but again said no. Eventually, another big bull saw his talent and agreed to let him participate in the production. Lesson learned.

Years later when he stumbled, as we all do, the Hollywood herd wanted to put him out to pasture. This Standing Bull summoned his inner bull and battled the label they branded on him. So, he directed another production. He tried something else. He worked hard. Success, he observed, requires working harder than you think you possibly can. You can't hold grudges, because it's counterproductive to your goal. You're going to get knocked down in life. All that matters is that you get back up. There's always honor in being a Standing Bull.

CHINA SHOP BULL

The China Shop Bulls are clumsy and lack finesse. Their style is rough, gruff, and often destructive. In 17th-century London, cattle were brought to the local market where shops were lined up on the main street. Sometimes cattle would wander into stores that sold fragile plates, glasses, and teacups, causing turmoil. In dealing with China Shop

Bulls, you have to tactfully distance yourself because you could be held responsible for their messes. Avoid reckless people.

BRAHMAN BULL

The Brahman Bulls make you reluctant to say no because they always trot out their high falutin' pedigrees to overwhelm you. However, there are many roads that lead to the rodeo. Abraham Lincoln and Lyndon Johnson never attended an Ivy League school, but were still in a league of their own. Eisenhower graduated at the bottom of his class at West Point but this five-star general pointed the United States in the right direction to win World War II—a far greater challenge than your office politics. Do you think Bill Clinton or Barack Obama spent much time around the country club while they were growing up? They did their learning elsewhere.

Trust your instincts and be prepared to use your connections to logic, kNOwledge, and innovation to succeed when you don't have all the branding.

BOB THE BULLY

Bob the Bully doesn't use brute force to terrorize at work. Instead, this gun-slinging, steely-eyed bull engages in verbal violence. He spreads rumors. He tries to ruin reputations. He uses exclusion as a tactic to lure lieutenants who are grateful for his attention. In groups, he will charm a fellow bull while snickering at how another bull isn't as smart as they are. Bob the Bully creates the illusion that he has the support of the majority, which instills the fear of speaking out in those who witness his cruelty. Soon, his behavior is tolerated and becomes the accepted norm of the group. Since he lacks empathy, demeaning and demoralizing people becomes a blood sport. Bob will come up with initiation rites, rallying songs, and pet nicknames; he'll even create exclusive outings to make his chosen group feel special. Unless someone challenges Bob's brutish behavior, it will persist. It is why bulls must remember that silence is a sound.

HENRY THE HOOFER

Henry the Hoofer plays it safe and never sticks up for anyone. He's often Bob the Bully's lieutenant. This bull never says, "No, this isn't right. No, let's try it this way." Nor does he even say yes.

He is a man of his most recent word, someone of little wit and much malice, who will sink any project in procedural molasses.

He doesn't want to commit to anything, whether it be a project, a person, or a cause.

As a boss, he wants to be agreed with even if it hurts the company's bottom line. If you present a project, he will shake his head, move his feet, and create clouds of dust to distract friends, colleagues, and bosses from your good ideas and desires. In his warped thinking, he figures that there are more terrible ideas than innovative ones, so obfuscate and BS. Create enough dust so nothing gets done.

As a date, he will lead you on with promises for years and never pop the question.

He's an expert at saying, "Let's discuss this tomorrow," though he never does. He is *not* to be trusted.

YELL-OW BULL

The Yell-ow Bull yells so much that it hurts. He's like a hard rock band playing next door while you're trying to sleep. This bull screams at everyone—employees, relatives, and innocent waitresses—justifying the abuse by claiming that it's their fault for not being smart enough. These types of bulls often have power positions because they are passionate about products and ideas. His booming voice resonates louder than everyone else's, especially when he goes bullistic. During a disagreement with this bull, many people will resort to their own defensive mode. Don't. If this bull raises his voice, don't raise yours. It will only escalate the fight. He likes and even respects being disagreed with, but only if you calmly state the facts. The more relaxed you are, the easier you can subdue this bull and work with him. He's loyal but difficult.

STRATEGIES TO BECOME BULLISH AT WORK AND EVEN MAKE A BULLION

We've now established the types of bulls that roam through our offices. In this section, we offer strategies to maximize our results while dealing with the often snorting, stinky, unbridled beasts that cause us problems.

[40]

Back in ancient Greece, women had to navigate roads filled with similar bulls. Legend has it that because they couldn't compete with brute strength, they learned a special dance where they would grab the bulls' horns and leap over them. It was an impressive feat and men got into the act, too. In time, the leapers became highly skilled (at least the ones that didn't get gored did) and could sense the perfect time to grab the horns so the bull would jerk his head upwards, giving the leaper added momentum to soar in the air. It was a spectacle to watch man and beast so in sync. These performances turned the dancers into stars. But they couldn't be successful, and neither can you, without following the right steps and trusting your animal instincts.

CARRY YOUR OWN LOAD

Many human bulls complain that their hard work isn't getting them anywhere. Often this is because they haven't said no to other tasks. They haven't realistically assessed how much time a task takes to be completed. Here's a bulletin from Bull-et Point John and Jane: If you think your time is limitless, you will say yes to everything and pay the price. Time management is essential for success because there are rarely any overnight successes and mostly up-all-night successes.

Write down a list of your daily tasks. Then write down how much time you think each task takes. Surprised? After a day or two, you will see that many human bulls do not have realistic projections. They end up exhausted from chasing their own tail and following everyone else's. Saying no enables you to save time, which you can instead devote to study and practice, the raw materials of achievement.

PRIORITIZE

Successful bulls prioritize. Instead of mentoring colleagues throughout the week, one bull became more productive by earmarking Friday afternoons for this project. Another learned that you don't have to overextend for every task as you did in high school and give all assignments an A+ effort. Save it for the important ones. When asked to compile research and arrange lunch for a meeting, one bull spent hours calling different restaurants in search of the finest wheatgrass juice. However, this left less time for research, the part of the job that gets the bull kudos. Prioritizing is like making deposits in a bank with certain tasks providing better returns.

Remember, not all tasks are of equal value. During World War I, British officers demanded their troops looked "bull," which meant a polished appearance. To the frustration of Australian and New Zealand soldiers who fought with them, the Brits would sometimes be more concerned about their military uniforms than combat strategy. As lexicographer Eric Partridge believed, the Australian and New Zealand soldiers started referring to this practice as "B.S." Don't waste your talent on distractions. It decreases effectiveness and undercuts real leadership and vision.

AUDIBULL

Bulls hear low and high frequencies better than humans do. Too often, human bulls spend time talking and not listening to what is behind someone's words. This is understandable. If you are bracing for conflict or rejection, you are busy thinking about your next move. You are waiting to hear the other bull's position and preparing an argument against it.

Always consider what the motivation is behind your bull's actions. What do they want and not want? What do you both have in common? We are so programmed to think, "Yes, this is what they want," that we often don't decipher what someone is really saying.

Two bulls were competing for a boss' approval to build a stall. Since nourishment is an obvious concern, they debated the size of the water trough, the type of food dispenser. For hours, they one-upped each other, bellowing about the latest high tech products in the market. In fact, the window was the most important concern because the boss wanted fresh air during the day. He didn't care whether the water trough was made of steel or wood.

Listen carefully to a boss or client's needs.

WE ARE ANIMALS, NOT COMPUTERS

Say no to making critiques personal. "You are not producing enough beef" is a statement that may be intended to identify a problem but will be heard as an attack. The egos of human bulls will become defensive and whatever brilliant solution you then say will not be heard. A better approach is saying: "Our company wants to produce more beef. Here's a new idea." Always separate the animal from the problem.

QUESTIONABULL

A bull likes to feel bullish. Asking his opinion only burnishes that feeling. Since we have established that bulls need to be respected, instead of saying no directly to a proposal, position it as a question and then offer how you could do it differently.

"Did I understand correctly what you are saying? Let me see if I can explain it from your perspective." Understanding your bull's point of view is not the same as agreeing to it. This is a common strategy for Sitting Bull, as well as the Brad Pitt Bull. By feeling understood, the bull at the other end of the negotiating table will better absorb your position without feeling threatened and will be more open to compromise.

Exploitabull

Some bulls go into meetings making concessions to cultivate the business relationship. "You want my stall? I'll give you that and my horn vest, too." Other bulls approach negotiations differently. They will make threats to achieve concessions. "If you don't give me this stall at $20, I am leaving." You, as a nicer bull, need to sell the stall but at what cost? Don't buy into the belief that there is only one buyer. You can use your creativity to rent the stall, turn it into a farm stand, or wait for another bull to come to pasture.

Don't be exploited. Have a number you won't budge on. Know when to say no and create limits to what is acceptable. Until the bull sees that part of your negotiating style, you can never have equal footing.

SHARPEN YOUR BULL HORNS

We all like to stretch. But keep your nose focused on what you are good at and keep the stretching for yoga class. Instead of volunteering for work that is out of your expertise, stay focused on your talents. If you are an architect, don't volunteer to do extra accounting work. This way you sharpen your natural strengths in building your professional future. After all, to become a master in any field, human bulls need to practice a skill for 10,000 hours.

How did Steve Jobs, the creator of Apple, develop the iPad, iPhone, and the company's other beloved products? He selected what *not* to put in a product. He resisted going off in many different directions and instead did a few things better than any other company.

"Focus is about saying no," he said, "and the result of that focus is going to be some really great products."

> "People think focus means saying yes to the thing you've got to focus on. But that's not what it means at all. It means saying no to the hundred other good ideas that there are. You have to pick carefully. I'm actually as proud of the things we haven't done as the things I have done. Innovation is saying no to 1,000 things."

> —STEVE JOBS, Apple Worldwide Developers' Conference, 1997

MARKET INTELLIGENCE

Often narcissists will ask for ideas and then take them as their own. Keep email trails of what you contribute. After meeting with a Bob the Bully or Brahman Bull, make sure you send an email of what was discussed. An example could be: "Since you liked my suggestion, here is more information." This puts all bulls on notice and gives you tangible proof of your contributions if needed later for company evaluations or when pursuing other jobs.

BOSSES ARE NOT YOUR THERAPIST

Know this: Your boss is not obligated to compliment you, because you are being paid for a job. Your paycheck is the reward. Keep conversations fenced around work issues. Keep hanky-soaking tears or daily dramas from the homestead out of the office.

Human bulls must know how to get their emotional needs met outside of work. In fact, most executive recruiters say that people who over-share personal information on interviews don't get the job. Personal challenges can be shared with friends, family, therapists, rabbis, pastors, and even the great bull in the sky—but not your boss.

SHOOTING THE BREEZE

It can come as a shock to learn how many people get promoted who, when compared to you, are not as smart or capable. It can also be a challenge to work with people every day whom you know to be conniving, or cunning, or who will stop at nothing to get ahead. How do you keep your integrity while trying to fit in with these bulls who have power over your paycheck and can influence your job status and reputation? You have to know when to say no. Be like Sitting Bull. Unless it is an ethical issue, resist the urge to correct or comment on people until you accumulate information on the players in your office as well as their strengths and weaknesses.

You will soon see how many corporate

bulls like Henry the Hoofer want a lot of yes men and women around them. They want the status quo guarded and will sabotage people who offer new ideas or ways of doing things. They are scared of change that may make them obsolete or expose their limited talents. Bosses also like to be admired and flattered. Very few are like Ronald Reagan, who proudly hired many people smarter than he was.

So take a cue from Sandy Bull-ock and the Brad Pitt Bull. Spend a little time making colleagues feel comfortable with you by suggesting news articles to read or seminars worth attending. Be bullish on substance and provide useful or amusing information. Hearing a funny story will humor even the toughest of bulls, along with the occasional compliment on a cool-looking tie or dress. Go to the company picnic. This creates goodwill and camaraderie so that when you make requests about job terms, project ideas, or vacation time, you will get it.

COLLEAGUES CAN SMELL FEAR

Bulls have an incredible sense of smell. They can detect odors five miles away. If bullies in your office smell fear or insecurity, they will take advantage. They feed on fear. People pleasers waste time trying to make these bulls their friend. They chase them down the office with a rose dangling from their lips and bile behind it. Deep inside you realize there is an imbalance in this relationship. Here's a little exercise. Every time you feel intimidated, repeat this bull whisperer mantra to yourself: "I am safe, healthy, wise, and strong." It really works.

Experts suggest using assertive body language to combat adult bullies. Look firmly in their eyes and stand straight. Also, use an authoritative tone of voice. Standing up to these bulls seems hard, but if you know that deep down they are cowards who use intimidation tactics, you can out-maneuver them or at least make them go elsewhere. You must say no to this bull or you will be a target. Find their weakness. Every bull has one. "No, I think this is a better way of doing it" will neutralize their attacks. You need a win with Bob the Bully.

Meanwhile, simultaneously start documenting examples of bullying behavior. Give facts, not feelings, about your complaints. "He hurt my feelings" is not the way to go. "He berated colleagues in a meeting who were offering ideas" is a far better approach.

In many corporations today, if others bulls complain about bullying behavior, managers will "ring-fence" the executive. These alpha bulls are considered more dangerous than those he or she is abusing and will be either ring-fenced or fired. If you speak up and tell the bully you may report him, he will also be more inclined to back down because no one can afford to be branded a bully.

CYBER-BULLIES

Cyber-bullies lash out more easily because they can cloak their viciousness by creating pseudonyms in chat rooms for gossip and slander. Most electronic forums lack supervision. Furthermore, once defamatory material is exposed on the Internet, it is difficult to remove and can go viral. Since 2007, seven states have passed laws against digital harassment and more will follow. The best strategy is to summon your inner bull and be part of the solution and not the problem. If you see mean-spirited dialogue, comment on it even when it is not about you. More than 80 percent of young people don't report the abuse. If you say, "What cowards people can be for writing malicious gossip," it will put other bulls on notice that you have the moral courage to confront it and are listening to the bull whisperers inside who encourage reaching for our better selves. As Teddy Bear Bull's niece Eleanor Roosevelt said, "No one can make you feel inferior without your permission." Conduct yourself as a stand-up bull. Both Teddy Bear Bull and Standing Bull will support you.

Chasing Away Bullies

Many have failed in business and life by underestimating the power and determination of others. Take, for example, the story of Civilón, the famous Spanish bull. Civilón had such a sweet disposition that children flocked to his owner's fighting bull ranch to feed him wildflowers and marvel at his gentle nature. As his fame grew, he was consigned to a bull ring in Barcelona right at the time the city was threatened by Franco's fascist forces. A promoter came up with the idea of pitting the pacifist bull against mounted picadors. Hundreds of fans lined the bleachers waiting to see if Civilón had the ability to summon his inner warrior when needed. When the picadors tried to lance him, Civilón resisted the aggression and instead charged after them, toppling horses one after another so that the picadors were chased behind the barricades. As a result of his bravery, Civilón got a rare reprieve from being killed. Civilón proved that being kind and caring is not weakness, but actually strength. Like most heroes, this type of strength has a ripple effect. Civilón, the hero bull, was later shipped back to his ranch awaiting a well-deserved retirement. However, on the night of July 18, 1936, Franco's bullies entered Barcelona looking for food and ransacked the bull ring stables. Civilón was killed and eaten for breakfast. This incident naturally made people sick to their stomachs. In fact, Civilón's remains nourished and activated the opposition to fight back against Franco forces and the date Civilón was eaten is often considered as the beginning of the full-scale Spanish Civil War.

Nor is it coincidental that a bull exposed the torment of this war in Pablo Picasso's famous 1937 painting, Guernica. Many in Spain were illiterate but were able to witness the horrors inflicted on villagers through Picasso's painting which remains one of the art world's most enduring anti-war symbols. In the mural, the bull isn't wounded and remains strong and virile. However, because of its proximity to a grieving mother, the bull is sympathizing with her pain and, with flared nostrils and angry eyes, becomes a witness judging the atrocities. Aside from his Guernica masterpiece, Picasso also used his beloved bull in 1945 to create a series of 11 lithographs to show the trajectory of realism to abstraction. This master class, as these works are called, methodically showed how by dissecting the lines of a bull and emphasizing different parts, one can discover the spirit of the beast and view the creature with fresh eyes.

The strength within is not always visible. But it is there, and when harnessed, is a potent force for good.

Be Honorabull

We all have a beast within us that is not our higher self. It is often fed with negativity, envy, fear, and greed. Fight the impulse even if those around you aren't as honorable. Being a good person has to happen when someone isn't looking because you never know who may be watching. As an example, look at what happened to King Minos, the offspring of Zeus and Europa. When Poseidon asked him to sacrifice a special bull, he substituted an inferior one. As punishment, his wife, Pasiphae, was tricked into siring the infamous bullheaded Minotaur, a nasty piece of work. Minos then found the craftsman Daedalus to build an elaborate labyrinth with multiple blind passages to imprison the monster. The monster was not only the son of Minos's wife but also the monster inside Minos himself, which had led him to abuse his public duty for increased personal gain. Many have so much and don't need more. Say no to cutting corners because you may then be lost in Minotaur's maze.

CREATE A BULLY PULPIT

Back in the 1900s, whenever someone received good news people actually remarked, "Bully for you." That's why Teddy Bear Bull used that term to create the bully pulpit.

In a competitive global market, successful

companies need the equivalent of bully pulpits. Companies like Google welcome ideas from everyone. The company has also worked hard to banish the perception that employees are meant to agree with the boss and the idea that saying no is disrespectful. Google has called this practice "the need for employee engagement."

As a result, employees have contributed to the success of the company by safely offering new ideas. The best way to accomplish this feat is for offices to have a bully pulpit with sets of rules so ideas are encouraged and not shot down. Start one. You will be looked at as a leader and the Teddy Bear Bull will be proud. Just don't call it the Bull Moose Party.

Motor Skills

Don't be fooled by appearances. There are bulls who can navigate a china shop as well as your business portfolios. Whether small or big, they have found ways to maneuver the narrow passageways, which is where opportunity often is found. Remember that iconic

Merrill Lynch ad? California ranchers spent three months leading a black Longhorn bull through a maze of crates and hay bales that simulated a china shop. Then the bull was ready for its close-up. During the 16-hour shoot, the bull steered clear of the expensive Baccarat glasses and Wedgwood china. The bull didn't even chip a teacup. The only damage was to a $3,500 candelabrum, which was accidently shattered when the set designer dropped it after the bull had left.

Quarterback and Receivers

All teams have different strengths. With the Texas Longhorns, a great quarterback needs a great receiver. On the Chicago Bulls, you need guards and forwards. Find colleagues that complement your skills and create teams. It not only protects you from the other charging bulls but also provides strength in numbers. Choose your human bull teammates based on qualities such as smarts, efficiency, and reliability. It's what bulls do. Cows excel at choosing leaders. Social

THE NEED TO SAY "NO"

hierarchies are formed with leaders chosen based upon intelligence. In fact, in groups of cattle of different ages, leaders are amongst the oldest, suggesting that experience is valued as a strength.

An Ancient Fable

In Indian mythology, Mahisa was a bull-shaped demon king who couldn't quite play nice with the other gods, each of whom had a unique power. Because Mahisa was becoming a dictator, the gods turned to their primal deities, Vishnu and Shiva, for help stopping Mahisa.

Shiva had a close relationship with the bull Nandi, but he detested Mahisa. At Shiva and Vishnu's prompting, all the gods surrendered their weapons, ornaments, and powers, which caused them to merge into a single flame. This flame in turn took on the shape of a goddess with 18 arms named Durga. Durga rode forth on a lion and issued a mighty roar as she announced her presence. The bull demon sent armies against her, which she slew with little effort. The bull demon threw a mountain at her and bellowed angrily, but Durga gracefully leapt onto the bull's back, kicked his neck with her foot, and struck with her trident. However, the lesson wasn't that Durga slew the bull demon; rather, the lesson lies in how the gods successfully responded to this threat. Individually, they could do nothing, but together they were able to combat the evil. The power of community is greater than the sum of its parts. Durga is the personification of a power within all of us, a power of which the gods had been unaware until they acted together. Create a good team around you.

WINNING

Winning is not crushing your opponent or making someone lose. Saying no to that impulse is being a wise bull.

Finding a way to compromise is winning. Any war has bloodshed and destruction on both sides that can't be won back. If you go to war, it shows that you didn't find a way for everyone to get what they needed. Neither party has to lose. That's how you win.

It's like bull riding. You ride for only eight seconds and get off. This way the spirit of neither man nor animal is broken.

PART IV

THE BULL
AT HOME

Among their strong points, bulls can bear heavy loads and don't mind being tethered to other animals, although they do prefer some to others. Their favorite pastime is eating and lying down. You gotta love that. More importantly, bulls don't mind being domesticated for farming, unlike the wild animals that roam other continents.

Civilization became more sophisticated and cooperative because man began to use cattle as workers. Increased crop yields allowed larger populations to form and develop other skills that helped the community grow. However, dealing with all these larger family relationships presents its constant challenges. There are always those who don't carry their own weight and expect you to take the load.

Sure, you've occasionally said no to siblings, parents, lovers, and your kids. But not nearly enough, and when you do, maybe it hasn't been too convincing. Here's how to change that.

KNOWING YOUR BULL SPOUSE

Dealing with a bullish spouse can be frustrating. They are easily defensive and quick to attack. If you are thin-skinned, this can be especially painful. You want to retreat into a cave with your bruised heart. While we may not agree with how our spouses behave, we should remember on some primal level that it was their toughness that most likely attracted us in the first place. At work they get respect for being tough and they often transfer that role to home. Charging into the house and ruffling your routine or critiquing the way you approach basic tasks can be upsetting. It can even activate the angry bull inside you. It's time to toughen up, reduce fired-up emotions, and find strategies that get better results. A loving bull sounds like an oxymoron but it is possible.

RITUALS

Life is so much better when you take pleasure in the small things.

When your spouse comes home, create a ritual that immediately separates work from home. It could be a glass of wine, some soothing music, scented candles, or snacks placed on a counter. Perhaps suggest a promise of five minutes without either of you talking about the kids. Or strategically share a clever story you read or a joke you may have heard or found on Google. A peck on the cheek can soften the toughest bulls. You want to establish with your bull that you are not an employee, but their beloved spouse and life partner.

COMMUNICATE WITH WORDS NOT ANIMAL SOUNDS

Most people who have problems saying no resort to other forms of communication. They pout, mope, whine, shuffle their feet, snort, or sulk. They feel pressure to do things they don't want to do, but the reality is they put the pressure on themselves. They are too often thinking about the things they should do or think people expect them to do. If you want to eat at a Tex-Mex restaurant, don't agree to dine at the French one. If you don't want to include your sister-in-law yet again on a family trip, say so. Chances are that your bull wouldn't be as upset as you think. Most things we worry about don't happen. Try saying no in a nice way and offering alternatives and you will see the results.

DRAWING THE LINE

If a line isn't drawn, boundaries are blurred. One cowering cowgirl complied with her spouse and stifled her true desires and opinions for 20 years, until the kids left for college. Then she filed for divorce, shocking her husband and family. Because of the lack of honesty, the relationship suffered and resentment metastasized into anger. If desires are not expressed directly, it causes a low-grade fever that lingers and eventually kills the relationship.

DIVISION OF LABOR

Bulls understand the importance of having a division of labor. But it's important to understand that these chores have to be discussed. In many marriages, one person feels that the other person isn't carrying their load. But have you articulated what is expected? If you don't ask, you don't get. One bull spouse may feel that providing food, shelter, sparkly presents on birthdays, and being the go-to kids' sports coach is taking care of his load, when in fact the other spouse wants different pick-me-ups—the dishes, for one; more affection and personal notes for another. Be specific. Instead of attacking and saying, "You don't . . .," which puts someone on the defensive, try to reframe your requests as, "I am happy when . . ." That is when you can make interior improvements that benefit the whole family.

BEING VULNERABULL

Too many of us expect our spouse to be mind readers. ESP would be great, but most need more TLC. When a bull criticizes you for not wearing a coat, you may interpret it as a judgment or an insult on your organizational skills, echoing a past criticism from your mother. In fact, he may just be worried about you catching cold, since in his past *his* mother almost died from pneumonia. Your reacting angrily makes him feel misunderstood. Most fights are caused by not considering the vulnerabilities behind our statements. In any exchange with your bull spouse, ask yourself what vulnerabilities are being triggered. We all have attachment injuries. Be tender and realize some wounds never fully heal. We just have to build the muscle around them with love, understanding, and acceptance. Say no to expecting perfection; not only in yourself, but also in your spouse. As one bull crooned, love me when I least deserve it because that's when I need it most. This makes a bull feel loved, safe, and loyal.

How to Become Forgivabull

Bulls fight with each other. It's what they do. Then they move on. When criticized, it is natural to become defensive. People don't like to admit they're wrong, especially when they may have come home too late, missed a birthday, or been self-absorbed instead of acting as a team player. Fight the primal instinct to BS and come up with a lame excuse. Saying, "I messed up; I'm sorry" shows courage and class. It also shortens the argument. Any marriage requires a combination of forgiveness—for the inevitable disappointments big and small—and the flexibility to accept that one day your bull spouse may like snoozing in the wilderness and another day may want to dance under the stars. We are travelers together, not always on the same train schedule. Think always of what you have and don't dwell on what you don't. The habits of another bull could be worse than yours. Have you ever heard a Longhorn snore?

TRAINABULL

If your spouse yells a lot, drinks too much, is chronically late, or can be very critical, you have a choice on how you react to these patterns of behavior. Instead of responding, "Stop yelling at me. You must be nicer." You can say, "You can continue to yell at me if you choose to, but I am choosing to not be in your presence until you speak to me respectfully." That's a boundary. That's saying no to behavior that upsets you.

THE NEED TO SAY "NO"

If your spouse remains deaf to your complaints, action will speak louder than words. Instead of stressing that your spouse is going to run late or be too tired to attend the barn dance, inform her that she can choose to leave later but you will be going to the event as scheduled. After a few times of leaving on time, your spouse will realize that her lateness is not tolerated and she has the choice to go with you or stay home. Notice that you are not demanding that your spouse do something. You are setting boundaries and standards of what you will do or will not do.

Speak Calmly

Those who rarely say no and finally do often feel suppressed anger flare up. They become like China Shop Bulls crashing through the home and causing destruction. They are red with rage from past hurts. Be aware of these patterns and police yourself. Words have power and can deliver fatal blows. You don't want your loved one to hear your anger

THE NEED TO SAY "NO"

without hearing your words. Take a deep breath and speak calmly while expressing your new boundaries and terms. The combination of clarity and calm is both seductive and effective.

Tongue Lashings

As one singer crooned, "It's hard to kiss the lips at night that have just chewed your ass out all day." Did you know that the tongue is made of the same tissue as the heart? The two are intrinsically connected.

After a long, tiring day, a spouse coming home from work was greeted with a mile-long list of chores. Fix the hayloft. Build a new fence. Wanting to avoid a tongue lashing, the spouse reluctantly agreed. But resentment was building like a deadly Kansas dust storm. He finally plucked up the nerve to say no. Some chores can and should wait for another time, and your no can be followed with a yes for a specified date in the future. You also can say no because you don't want to do a chore. As Dr. Henry Cloud counsels, you are not a human appendage to fulfill all the needs and wants of your partner at that very moment. Saying no without the other person feeling that you are listening is absorbed as an emotional punch. But saying no while making clear that you have considered their feelings won't breed misunderstanding or resentment. All marriages need the clause, "We agree to disagree on this one."

BEING CHANGABULL

Loved ones can be very confused when suddenly you change the path you have been leading for many years. You have to give them a new map. You have to give them direction. Since this bull is someone you love, understand that your bull's natural defensiveness will activate. If your bull raises their voice, don't raise yours. Use a special nickname or a loving endearment that only you two share to make your bull feel safe that you want to take this road together. After all, most bulls attack out of fear. People are instinctively resistant to change. They shake their heads, groan, and get cranky. Position your desires as a route for bettering both your lives. Compare it to taking out crayons and creating enough colorful experiences to paint a Montana sunset.

Be Patient

Anything good takes time. And persistence. Try not to get too frustrated when it seems your bull isn't as responsive as you'd like. Your stamina will be tested because many people don't take no for an answer. Like salesmen, they think no is the beginning of a pitch to convince you to say yes. You must be firm. Push back and ask that your choices be respected. If you are a role model in being happy with the direction your life is now taking, it usually rubs off. If it doesn't, you can go in different directions and cultivate what you still have in common. No matter how slow your progress, you are still way ahead of everyone who isn't even trying. The wisdom of the bull tells us that your life doesn't change by chance, but from actively making changes.

Rolling In the Hay

In many marriages, when someone doesn't say no enough in other parts of their relationship, they often say no to sex where they feel they have control. When the motivation is to punish versus love, it creates an echo chamber of confusion and resentment. In a relationship, pleasing your partner and receiving pleasure is part of the give and take. It should not be an act of submission. But neither should it turn into an act of abandonment. Intuitively you know the difference.

Don't Love Out Of Fear

In Vedic Indian history, when the sacred bull bellowed, cows would flock to its pure sound. These bulls would put out a vibration of their essence, in tune with the universe, which attracted support from invisible sources. The Vedic breath—which most people know from meditation as *om*—infuses practitioners with inner fullness, not fearfulness. In a way, that is what someone who finally expresses their true self is doing. It is both a calling and an opportunity. If you are brave enough to say goodbye, life will reward you with a new hello. The person who lives in fear that someone will leave lives in constant anxiety. There's no peace. It is honorable to sacrifice and deny yourself for the sake of others, but only if it is coming from a place of strength. When you become a Standing Bull and stand for something, you will be rewarded. It may take time, but it will come.

Bringing Out the Best Bull

We all need alone time. Take the occasional trip away. Earmark time to be with friends for a frolic on the beach. Go for a bike ride. Play poker with your pals on Thursday night.

Back in the age of Zeus, a wandering bull known as Cerus terrified people because he would periodically trample villages and no one could stop him. The bull was wild and out of control, choosing to run with his emotions. One day the goddess of spring, Persephone, found him after he had trampled on a beautiful field of bloomed flowers. She spoke to him and though he couldn't understand the words, her presence calmed him. They formed a bond. The bull learned impulse control and patience and how to use his strength wisely. Persephone returned to the land every spring, and Cerus joined her. She sat upon his back and he ran her through the fields, allowing her to set all of the plants in bloom as they rode by. In the fall when Persephone returned to Hades, Cerus rode back to the sky as the Taurus constellation. Some bulls need more breathing space away from each other to make the relationship flourish and last.

A NOTE ON SAYING NO TO ANGRY BULLS

Bulls who are controlling and abusive don't accept no easily and require a different strategy. In fact, they can easily become more dangerous when they've been denied something they want. A no can be perceived as a deliberate provocation; a waving of the flag, triggering the bull to charge. Domestic violence groups warn victims not to leave until they have strategized an exit plan—to a family member's home, a shelter, a church, or a synagogue. Preparation is essential for safety. Although well-meaning friends may have told the victim to just say no countless times, the fact is that this bull has most likely fenced out all interactions with loved ones over time. The victim is dazzled at first by all the attention and the bull's desire to monopolize all free time. The victim gradually loses their ability to be independent and accepts the abuse in exchange for love. This is a form of control, not love. In all interactions with angry bulls, timing is critical to success.

KNOWING YOUR BULL CHILD

When children devise fanciful tales, we often think it is wildly cute and inventive. We admire their vivid imaginations and smile at their ingenuity. We forgive them. This acceptance and even affection can reinforce the behavior. In a way, stretching the truth is supported by loving parents from the earliest days onward. But as little bulls grow up, this isn't as tolerable because BS has a shelf life. However, parents may still engage in supporting this form of storytelling. Out of primal, blinding love, mothers and fathers can overstate the competency of their children.

We even crave this type of praise, because somewhere deep in the recesses of our souls, we sense greatness in ourselves that has never surfaced or been recognized by others, and it feels good that Mom or Dad see it so clearly. It gives us hope for potential. But we have to fulfill that potential with hard work and, eventually, realistic appraisals of our talents. Try to see yourself as others do and not only through your parents' eyes. Furthermore, there are bulls who not only expect the world to treat them as a beloved child forever, but also expect their parents to always rescue them. Thanks to misguided love, they have never encountered obstacles or judgments. They have never heard the word no and are paying the consequences.

The baby bulls who grow up in the wilderness with falling branches and adversaries know how to fend for themselves and can anticipate danger. They know how to be resourceful and inventive. They don't just recite what they learned in a book.

> "I am thankful to all those who said no. It's because of them, I did it myself."
>
> —ALBERT EINSTEIN

The bulls who expect parental love in the adult world are in for a rude awakening. They are either too impatient for approval and promotion, or are not willing to work and fight for a place in the pecking order.

Here are ways to give your child a strong backbone so they can withstand the assaults

and attacks, both verbal and physical, which
will happen in the bullpen of life.

You Have to Say No and Mean It

A wise bull responsible for running a major
media empire has five successful daughters.
Friends ask him what he did, what his secret
was. First, he credits his wife, who shares the
secret. You must pick an issue on which you
plan to be as stubborn as a bull. No cell phone
until 10 years old. No ear piercing until 16.
And stick to it. Then, for one infraction they
may have committed, make sure you enforce
an appropriate punishment and stick to it.
Talking back means a vacation is canceled.
The little bulls will whine and complain. But
they will learn that no means no. They will
respect you. So, afterwards, when daddy bull
says that if you choose to do this, there will
be consequences, they won't doubt him. They
will make better choices. And they will learn
delayed gratification. Pick something to say

no to with a promise of a yes in the future to teach discipline and values.

EXPLORE YOUR VALUES

Breeding matters. Ask any person who works with bulls. There's value in knowing where you come from and what you stand for. Human bulls need to fill their little bulls' ears with dinnertime stories about how they are part of a big bullpen. The little bulls need to be reminded that they are linked to their ancestors: aunts and uncles, grandmothers and grandfathers. That they can derive guidance from a value system that cares about loving hearts, curious minds, a strong education, and helping those in need. Tell them stories about the challenges and failures of relatives as well as the triumphs. This also helps them develop the strength to say no to bad behavior and peer pressure. Using the words "in this family we value" instead of "you must" will make your kids less inclined to break rules—and less inclined to break your heart in the process.

DISCIPLINE VERSUS PUNISHMENT

Bulls are disciplined creatures that know they must keep their herd moving forward. The wise bull knows that discipline is not punishment. It is not a payment for a wrong. It is the building of an internal value system.

Punishment looks back. It pays for wrongdoings in the past. Discipline looks forward in giving your bull child a structure to be more effective in their lives, to say no to too much promiscuity, alcohol, and unfulfilling relationships. Discipline means saying no to going to the movies so you can practice your batting swing, or your piano lesson. You have to say no to things to learn the benefits of discipline and see the rewards. Parental bulls can lead by example. How? By watching you resist going to a party so you can learn computers to improve your job performance, by seeing you work out at the gym to fight that belly fat, by observing you saying no to the apple pie on weekdays but giving yourself a treat on weekends—all these values get baked into their DNA.

ACCOUNTABULL

A little bull eyes a candy bar at the store. His mother says no. The little bull starts whimpering. He starts begging. Mama bull holds her ground. He then stomps his feet and yells at the top of his lungs, a full-throttled, glass-shaking scream. Mama bull caves. Convincing herself that it's just one candy bar, she justifies her response. As the little bull gets older, he realizes this tactic is effective and uses it for getting riding boots, bicycles, and later a pickup truck. Once the bull gets his license, he drives very fast. He gets speeding tickets. But Papa Bull pays for them. The young bull gets more speeding tickets and others for texting, and goes to court. Mama Bull hires a lawyer so his license isn't revoked. A few months later, the young bull dies in a car accident. Looking back, the parents now wish they would have put on the brakes and let him lose his license, instead of his life. Don't create the illusion of an omnipresent parent who will pick up all the slack. Encourage your little bulls, but let them experience consequences—or you will.

BANKABULL

Some adult child bulls become so accustomed to your saving them that they will stampede through your savings. Because you haven't said "no" enough, they expect you to clothe them, pay for new stalls, and even finance their fledgling business. You have given so much that you've put yourself at risk. When your adult child bull asks you for a loan, make sure you can afford it. That's not withholding love, it's protecting yourself. Give only what you can afford. Be available to help without jeopardizing your future. You can offer to help them get a bank loan, find additional chores raking hay, comb the Internet looking for foundations. You can even come and help paint a new office. But don't let them milk your bank account dry.

TETHERED

Some bulls actually want their children to be tethered to them. They want to control love out of loneliness or insecurity. In a tight economy, an adult bull child was offered a job in a new city with the promise of promotion and a better paycheck. This exciting news was greeted by his family with a demand that he not take the position. "After all I've done for you, how could you even think of leaving this city and me?" cried the mother bull. It is understandable that parents will miss their children. It is not understandable to hold a noose over their adult child's head to keep them in place. A child owes their parents gratitude and love, not the obligation to be at their beck and call. Parents need to respect that each bull has its own destiny.

SAFE SUFFERINGS

The great bulls pass on their knowledge to their little ones. By the time the little bulls leave the range, they take responsibility for their lives. They know that they can either say yes or no to choices that are presented to them. They know their success or failure is up to them. They don't blame others for their mistakes. They get what they get; they don't get upset. They know that they are winners for trying. They also learn from hearing the word "no" that they don't get everything they want in life. They learn to be grateful instead of entitled. Having heard the word no, they learn to be patient, self-sufficient, and appreciative. They learn that they are the architects of their own happiness.

KNOWING YOUR BULL FAMILY

Bulls remain very close to their family of origin but they also feel free to roam without judgment. Human bulls could learn these lessons as well.

Accepting the cycles of life is an essential ingredient to a satisfying life. In mythology, bulls are a lunar symbol because their horns look like crescent moons. Because the cycle of life is seen in the moon, going from dark to light, each new month offers the possibility of a rebirth. In fact, cattle, like humans, have 10-month pregnancies.

In a parent-child relationship, there are also many cycles from birth to adulthood. As children, we learn about the world through our parents and our own discoveries at school with teachers, friends, and colleagues. Although we sometimes may disagree with our families, we are still connected by blood and remain loyal to the herd, which includes our brothers and sisters.

The situation becomes more difficult when as adults we want to be viewed as the individuals we've become and not as the image our families may have of us. Our growing sense of self may also collide with the expectations of our family. We love our parents and siblings and will be there for them, but we also have other responsibilities that now must be considered. At times, this can cause a lot of angst, especially if we are dealing with a family member who is stubborn, critical, unappreciative, and bullheaded.

Here is how you can take the bull by the horn.

THE GOLDEN CALF

Honor thy parents, says the Ten Commandments. Did you notice that in that biblical passage, the word is honor, not love? Moses was very clear that you should follow the commandments and not that golden calf. Talmudic scholars interpret that choice of word as an important distinction. Love has to be earned. We are obligated to make sure our parents who raised us are taken care of. But we can say no to criticism and unwelcome demands. You do not have to be a child who is led on a rope as an adult. You have choices.

THE GOOD CHILD

In any family dynamic, each child is branded early. The nice one. The smart one. The pretty one. The one who will do everything for everyone. They get complimented. "You are so capable and kind." There's pride in being helpful. But not in being manipulated. "You're so capable that I told Mom to live with you." Everyone should carry their own load and contribute to their family. Don't let a relative exploit your good nature. Create a plan to share the burden.

RECONSTRUCTION

How do you build new fences? Like any carpenter, you need a tool kit.

First, you have to decide on location.

That's a key point in discussing any conflict or misunderstanding with a family member.

Schedule a rendezvous in a universally friendly place. Do not communicate over text or email. The emotional nuances can't be expressed properly through technology. You need this conversation to happen face-to-face. When in nature, away from technology, creativity is boosted over 50 percent. Choose a soothing place, like a meadow with fragrant lilacs or a rippling stream a stone's throw from your house. Or you can choose one of the many restaurants where the bull is featured, whether at the Cock 'n Bull or the Bull Valley Roadhouse. The bull's guidance is quietly all around us. So, next time you need to schedule a meeting, consider a place with the bull's name etched on it so that he can guide you towards your goal.

STAKES

When putting down the stakes to your fence, don't hammer too hard. If you hit too hard, the wood splits and so will your family member. It's a conversation with the goal of a better, closer relationship, not an attack or monologue. State what boundaries you now want to create.

One human bull had a brother who camped out at her summer cabin and was a slob. "I plan on staying a week at your house," he declared, never considering the inconvenience on his sister who had a busy workweek. Instead of feeling fenced in, the sister said, "No, at this time it is not convenient, but you can visit on this future date." She also took the advice of a wise bull who suggested she compose a Bull Manifesto for all houseguests regarding mealtimes, laundry, and expectations. A boundary was finally created. Sure enough, the next time the brother visited, he was more respectful and appreciative.

You Can't Be at Someone's Beck and Call

Say no to electronics for certain periods during the day. Interruptions can stall your career and your life. It breaks the flow of focus and the execution of thinking and perfecting. Like clockwork, your mom or sister calls as you're leaving for work or sitting down to dinner. Instead of saying, "No, I can't talk," you listen patiently as they complain about your nephew's basketball coach, your sister's bad haircut, or your mother's mahjong game. Inform your friends and family that you can speak only at specified times, such as during lunchtime or near bedtime. Most likely they'll find someone else to call and you won't be late or miss out on valuable time with your family.

REMIND YOUR PARENTS THAT YOU HAVE YOUR OWN FAMILY TOO

Vulnerabilities make people selfish. Bull parents sometimes forget that though their lives have slowed down, yours has revved up—even when you're not drinking Red Bull. There are the kids, your job, your leaking roof, carpooling, cooking, and squeezing in some friend time. You are not responsible for someone else's loneliness. Nor is it your job to be their entertainment. You are still a good person if you don't leave your son's baseball game because your father wants skim milk even though he has cream at home. Say no to leaving the game and yes to investing in an Internet or cable plan, or encouraging them to take educational classes at a community center.

BULL SESSIONS

When sharing your feelings, be warned. Bulls may get defensive with denials and will spew an avalanche of rebuttals. Resist the temptation to engage in accusations. Focus on the problem, not the person. Stray away from "You made me . . ." to another approach such as "I want to have a better relationship with you." By stating that you should have been more open and expressive about your feelings earlier, you prevent the other bull from feeling attacked. Owning that you have made mistakes in managing your familial relationships creates room for discussion rather than accusations. This way the bull will feel at ease with you and you both can lead the conversation to a mutual goal. Monologues are not conversations. Invite suggestions to better your relationship. Who knows? They may have a good suggestion.

SMILE

A bull's brain has as many folds and connections as a human brain and bulls also remember faces and events. For those who seek to avoid conflict or confrontation, expressing their needs can trigger stress instead of confidence. Controlling people will recognize this stress and use it to their advantage. The brains of human bulls can be influenced by smiling. Our brains register smiles as an emotion when we are not threatened. Over time, that message evolves so the muscle activity involved in a big warm smile sends a message to the brain signaling safety, which then translates into lower heart rates and stress levels. A warm smile can also thaw the coldest of bulls.

FAMILY RECIPES

Our families teach us who we want to be and who we don't want to be. Dealing with any family member requires managing expectations. Because anytime you argue with reality, you will lose. Know the bulls around you and what they are capable of, and don't try to change them. Instead, change how you react to them. Sometimes (like a time tunnel) they will swoop you back to that moment your sister ruined your favorite shirt, your dad called you lazy, your mother forgot to pick you up at school. You become stuck in that moment and deny yourself and your immediate family the best of you. You can't give the past that much power to impact the potential of your life. Too many people spend their adulthood recovering from their childhood. Don't set yourself up for disappointment and expect people to show gratitude and love as you do. You may think that true love is the measurement of how much someone is willing to be inconvenienced for you during a crisis. Others may think they've done their share by calling you once. Each person's ability to love and show love is different. Some have a gallon's worth, while others are at capacity with a pint.

SEE THINGS IN A NEW WAY

Discovered in 1994, France's Chauvet Cave is a maze of paintings and sculptures of bull depictions created 32,000 years ago—some of the world's oldest known art. A movement of the light source can cause the images to appear, while another makes them disappear back into the dark. If you want to see these images, you must make the effort to maintain a posture that keeps the light source in a certain position. You have to be focused to see the art. Stepping out of how you regularly see your family members can be similarly enlightening. Pretend you are meeting them for the first time. What would you say? How would they describe themselves? What are they the most proud of? Think of what you could discover about each other if the past wasn't in your present. Perhaps consider starting your relationships with a blank slate.

STRENGTH AND PEACE

Habits are like artistic patterns drawn on the inside of your body: They are colored by your experience and shape how you react and interact with the world. But you can redraw those lines with patience, observation, and creativity.

In the deepest part of the 1,700-foot Chauvet Cave, a cone of rock comes down from the ceiling to about a meter above the floor. The painting on the cone is known by archeologists as the *Venus of Chauvet*. A woman's pregnant belly is linked to a bull with her leg becoming his and his eye where her navel would be. The Venus and the bull are one, intertwined, connected, influencing each other.

Other cave excavations have revealed similar symbolism—the Laussel Venus holding her pregnant belly and the bullhorn, the pregnant La Madeleine Venus reclining next to a painted bull while another goddess rests her foot on the animal for support. There's another goddess, Astarte, revered in Greek and Hebrew cultures, who is always seen with the bull and a dove. Her message resonates today in any dealings with family members. While you are summoning your strength, you must always have your eye towards peace.

KNOWING YOUR BULL FRIENDS

As the wise Irish bull George Bernard Shaw once said, "You can't pick your family but you can pick your friends." We do choose our friends. However, sometimes we don't make the best choices. We may give human bulls our loyalty, our love, our time, and our secrets, but they have been known to turn on us. With sharpened horns, they can slash our hearts and our trust. They can disappoint. With no respect for history, they can heartlessly dispose of us when we are no longer useful to them. Here are some tips on gauging your friendships and finding ones where laughter erupts more than tears. After all, great friends are like a big soft bed of hay that cushions any fall and nourishes us with giggles and good times.

MENTAL TUNE-UP

Before you diagnose yourself with depression or self-doubt, make sure you are not surrounding yourself with cow dung. The reason you may have difficulty saying no is because you are surrounded by selfish narcissists.

Takers love givers. They're quick to say thank you but not to volunteer favors. But these bull friends have no problem asking to borrow your car, your brand new dress, those new golf clubs, or your father-in-law's contact at the law firm. They are so self-centered that it doesn't occur to them that they are not givers. Nor do they miss you if you leave because they are never truly attached to anyone. It's not personal. It's who they are.

So maybe it's time to swallow a bitter pill. You need a prescription to heal the discomfort you feel inside. The best medicine is a mental tune-up. Examine why you care about this person. What does this bull trigger inside you to make you want to overextend yourself for so little return?

Thanks to cattle, more than 100 medicines are available to human bulls, including estrogen and insulin. If being overly helpful to ungrateful people makes you sick inside, stop. Heal yourself by finding other people who share your values of friendship.

Don't Control Love

Is it possible that maybe you've made it too easy for the person you love to do nothing?

"I'll pick up your dry cleaning, make restaurant reservations, organize your kid's birthday party." These can be disguised attempts to control love. Back off a moment and see if your bull friend notices.

Relationships shouldn't be one-sided. If a bull puts all his weight on one foot, he will topple over. You are worthy of having someone want to please you, too. Use your bull's-eye to cultivate people who love you back.

PASSIVE-AGGRESSIVE BULL

Some bulls present their demands with cheerful enthusiasm. "You must come with us this weekend, you can't say no," puts pressure on a friend. The implicit threat is that if you say no, you will not be invited back to the group activity. Fearing abandonment is not a reason to cave in. Facing the facts of a tight schedule allows you to make choices that work for you and your family. Resist peer pressure at any age. Say no in a polite way and offer an alternative.

Often, these human bulls will also make commentary on your friends who may not be part of your group. "How can you be friends with that bull!" they snort. Recognize that these raging bulls strategically diminish others in order to make themselves appear more powerful. Your response must not be silence. Develop a strategy such as, "I can find something interesting in everyone. Can't you?" or, "She's always been a good friend to me." Put the attacking bull on the defensive and, if possible, do it publicly. Another bull once responded to this comment by saying, "Of course I like being with you the most but, when you're not available, we occasionally see each other since we both love to hike." Even if the other bulls don't register a response, they know that you had a backbone which gains respect. Another way to cultivate positive group dynamics is to become the consummate entertainer and organizer. Then you can choose what friends to invite to your soirees, barbecues, and gatherings. Making this effort also presents the possibility of introducing other bulls to each other and sparking new friendships.

BURNED OUT

Look for traps. Some friends will ask you for a favor without fully divulging how much time the task requires. "Come on, it will be fun," they'll say, as an enticing invitation. Some charity events require quarterly commitments versus monthly ones. Agreeing to bake a cake for a school auction is less demanding than running the fundraising committee. Always ask whether the commitment is long- or short-term and what the expected duration of the obligation is. None of us wants to disappoint. Saying no is often better than over-committing and not being able to deliver. Nor do we ever want to be called unreliaBULL.

HONESTY IS THE BEST POLICY

Want to impress a hostess? Say no without her having to hound you with emails and texts as though on a fox hunt. Too many human bulls wait until the last minute to respond to an invitation, which is both rude and annoying. It also forces the hostesses to scramble to determine how many provisions are to be served and prevents them from inviting other, more appreciative, guests. If you can't accept the invitation, say no. Embrace the person while declining the request. Hostesses appreciate it. And you'll get invited back.

WHEN YOU HAVE TO SAY NO TO A REQUEST

When someone asks us a favor, the kind bull in us wants to be helpful. But credibility is important, as is consideration for our other friend's time. An aggressive bull knows how to push the envelope of politeness. He'll say, "Call your friend and ask them if me and my fun and crazy bulls can crash at their summer rental." That's not stepping over, but crashing through a boundary. Sometimes pushy bulls ask you to send resumes to people you know for jobs they may not be qualified for. You are still a good person if you say that you are not comfortable with the request. Push back. "No, I don't feel comfortable calling my friend for this, but I'll try to think of someone else for you in the future." You are saying no to the request but not to your desire to help. Generous and kind bulls do try to link people together where it's mutually beneficial and without taking advantage of someone's valuable time.

A PACK CAN PROTECT YOU

Maintaining strong values requires being in a herd of supportive bulls. When you separate, it is hard to be disciplined and exercise self-control. It's better to keep in a pack of bulls with your value system, whether that is in a church, temple, yoga studio, or AA meeting. We need community.

One of Aesop's fables touches on a similar theme. A lion has his eye on three bulls in a pasture, but he is afraid to take them on together. Using guileful speech and spreading jealousy, he manages to separate them, then attacks successively without fear as they graze alone. The lesson is that we need each other and good bulls should stick together.

"The art of leadership is saying no, not yes. It is very easy to say yes."

—TONY BLAIR,
Former English Prime Minister

PART V

NEW PASTURES

After a long journey, bulls will stop at watering holes. Bulls wade in the water. They don't drown. They know exactly how deep to go, just like they know exactly how much they can carry. If it's too much, they say no. It's part of bull wisdom.

Yet human bulls allow themselves to swim in so much misinformation that they are drowning from it. We are up to our collective necks in BS, gasping for air, as data and drivel gush through every portal, competing for attention at supersonic speed.

That is why the bull whisperers are trying to give us a gentle wake-up call. The more we allow politicians and lawyers, as well as certain relatives, to happily stomp around on lies like they are starring in *Riverdance*, the more we are risking our future.

Sure, politicians have always spun the truth, salesmen have exaggerated a product's merit, men and women have embellished stories about sports or bedroom conquests. But there was always an expectation—something factual had to be supporting the bravado. As part of the game, everyone had their own personalized BS meter to gauge the amount of fact from fiction.

As long as you could distinguish, it was viewed as entertainment or part of commerce. Those who excelled got the label of BS artist, an acknowledgement of an art form. If someone had labored too hard or fabricated lies, they were dismissed as being full of it. The lines were drawn, which is what the bull whisperers encourage.

In the past decade, those lines have been blurred and boundaries mangled. The information highway no longer requires truth because we are not seeing enough consequences result from lies.

To win a primary, politicians cater to fringe groups and then, in an act of election schizophrenia, declare they've altered their views for the moderate majority. They demand a free pass to become centrists, telling us to believe what you hear until they change their mind.

In the office, a misinformed malcontent

with a keyboard can drown out honest, credentialed professionals, who care about accuracy and unbiased reporting.

Adding to the confusion is how those Red Bulls, along with some human scientists, will tell you that caffeine is great for you, while another unsubstantiated study will disagree and be given equal footing. Listen to Bull-et Point John and Sitting Bull. Sources matter. There is a difference between getting medical information from the Mayo Clinic versus sites peddling dubious information and products.

That is why you are being given a personal bullhorn to say enough is enough. Not to retreat and move backwards, but rather a willingness to turn towards a new direction—north towards the soul is always nice—or where the heart beats with a feeling of purpose and pride. This can happen only if you fight the fear and say no to BS and get bullish about substance. When it comes to life as well as love, illness, and even death, we are all amateurs. Our mission: learn survival skills to become the best we can be, while maintaining our integrity. As daunting as it can seem, authenticity is achieved by hundreds of little daily steps. Patience, smarts, and fortitude can and will lead to greener pastures.

PAPAL BULLS

Perhaps you may want to create your own papal bull to remind you of your goals. What is a papal bull?

Whenever the pope of the Catholic Church announces an issue of public importance in a letter, it is sanctified with a *bulla* seal. Technically, the bulla is a seal but that doesn't mean the bull spirit isn't involved here.

Although papal bulls were in use since the 6th century, the term became indoctrinated into the culture in the 15th century when one of the Vatican's offices was named "the register of the bulls."

And have no doubt; there were both bull-fights and some stubborn bulls in that group. On a spiritual level, the bull seal was the confirmation that the decree was authentic.

Consciously or unconsciously, many popes had a special feeling for bulls. In 1567, Pope Pius V issued a papal bull condemning bull-fighting as did subsequent popes in 1846 and 1940.

THE TEN BULLISMS

In the spirit of bull wisdom, here are ten bullisms discussed in this book. You can also add on your very own papal bull decrees for further inspiration and guidance.

1. Saying no means we have the skills to be bullish and not bullied.

2. Saying no means we are not addicted to the approval of others and have developed self-respect.

3. Saying no to rushing through life enables us to be more reflective and successful.

4. Saying no creates a sound that silences injustice and paves the way for change and innovation.

5. Saying no doesn't cause abandonment but possibility.

6. Saying no stops moochers from wanting to milk us for everything we have.

7. Saying no means we understand that even though there are many in need we can't successfully help everyone who asks.

8. Saying no means we are realistic about what is required to take care of ourselves and others.

9. Saying no can happen at any time. Even after you say yes, you can change your mind if your inner bull encourages you to change course, and you should trust this wisdom.

10. Saying no means we accept the yin and yang balance of the universe and how it is as essential and perfect as saying yes. After all, a contented life, as the wise bull knows, is the balance between holding on and letting go.

THE NOBULL PRIZE

Like a gust of wind, the bull's breath can push out the negative and bring in the positive. Wind, as you know, can't be seen, but it is felt. Remember the last time you may have said something out of fear or the desire for acceptance that wasn't totally truthful and you felt a zap inside? That's the bull's breath telling you to do better. To be more substantive and clever—even if it means having to work harder at tasks you may not like.

Emotions are like weather patterns in many ways. One moment it is sunny; another, stormy; sometimes a fog sets in blinding you.

Did you know that bulls have better forecasting abilities than TV meteorologists?

THE NEED TO SAY "NO"

Cattle can sense when it's going to rain and how hard. What do they do? They lie down in the fields and use the time for thinking and planning. They know when to fight the rain and when to wait until it passes. Bulls understand timing.

By summoning and trusting your inner bull, you can function with the world at large more effectively with strength, clarity, and industriousness. You can at last be bullish with life. And when you can roam the world with your values intact and your skills sharpened, you could be eligible for the NoBull prize.

THE MOST IMPORTANT NO

No fair is one of the most important phrases that can spill from any bull's lips. It is the battle cry of the young, who are often more concerned with combating injustice than many of the elders. Too often, older bulls that have been battered or numbed by seeing life's unfairness stray and become self-involved, interested only in their own families and friends. However, saying no to injustice is essential for leaving a legacy to our children and the world.

No fair is what drove Rosa Parks to say she wouldn't sit at the back of the bus during a time of segregation. *No fair* is what prompted Oprah Winfrey to demand fair pay to a man at her office. *No fair* is what motivated Jeffrey Wigard to expose toxins in cigarettes, Frank Serpico to speak out against police corruption, Daniel Ellsberg to expose government misdeeds, and courageous politicians to support bills that help the country and their communities not to succumb to bullying by political parties telling them how to vote.

Where do these inspiring people come from? They are all around us.

They are the bulls who have experienced the sting of whips as well as the crushing blows on their spirit and body from oppressive governments and dictators and find the courage to cry out and say no more.

They are the bulls who observe injustice outside their community and try to help even though it doesn't directly affect them. The bulls who give money or volunteer to worthy causes after a hurricane devastates a community, a storm uproots homes, or a person sits in jail unjustly. The bulls who are doctors and take care of uninsured people, the businessmen who help build a library, medical center, or affordable housing.

But there are human bulls who create small and big acts of moral courage every day. They say no to BS in the nicest way. As one of the great human rights leaders pointed out, "Moral courage means standing up not just to governments and armies, but to friends and families. It is the willingness to be ostracized by your community for what you believe is right."

To realize that silence is a sound. Yes, silence is a sound. It is a sound that helps the tormentor, not the victim. And when we do not say no, that act will define us, mark us like a scar.

Saying no to apathy and indifference liberates us. It gives us the freedom to leave a legacy. It gives us a shield to stand up to all the BS and instead spread seeds of love, valor, and fellowship.

Moral courage is what each of us is called upon to activate every day. Because every time you hear a sexist joke or a racial slur, every time you hear someone being talked down to or taken advantage of, you must make a decision. Will I be a perpetrator, a victim, a bystander, or someone who is part of the solution to make our world a better place? Will I be bullish or bullied? And each time you make the decision on which role you will play, you are exercising a muscle. Like any muscle, the more you use it, the stronger it becomes. And its strength defines us.

Because the bull is always watching.

BULLISH AND LOVABULL

Not everyone is a big bull. You don't have to be a CEO to see that the world is full of abundance, with different opportunities and pleasures. Bulls think about what they have and not what they don't. They squeeze the joy in life from small things. They know how to remain curious and teachable. They live in the moment and pride themselves on great work and moral values. They take it one step at a time. They accept their place in the world and the randomness of life because they know that greatness every day is achievable by anyone. Because as Christianity teaches, being of service to others is a door to greatness. Judaism encourages *tikkun olam*, the repairing of the world through the actions of each of us every day. Bull-loving Buddhists don't sugarcoat reality. They not only accept truth and all its ugly frustrating parts but also completely embrace it to the point that they can only laugh at life's endless absurdities. If we open our eyes, you will see how the bull has willingly been of service to mankind in countless ways, showing us how to better improve our lives and spirits.

How can we all do that? You know.

With love of course. You love the beast and the beast becomes a thing of infinite beauty, of possibility, excitement, passion, and rebirth. You mistreat it and the beast becomes darker and uglier, and so do you. It is consumed with envy, anger, and greed. The world sees you the way you see yourself.

So spread the word far and wide! Tell all your friends to stampede through the streets of their cities and towns like the bulls of Pamplona in a parade of sheer confidence and open-hearted vision that only a true bull person could understand.

There is a power in the herd. Because eventually the herd becomes its own single organism. It becomes one. One very powerful one. The truth is, your heart beats more powerfully, your courage is greater, and all the mistakes in life are far easier to accept when there is someone to take you into their arms and reassure you that you are part of the bigger picture. Everything you do matters.

So it's time to dig deep and free our inner bulls in an effort to rejoin our hearts and our herds. Sooner or later you reach that crossroad moment that offers you a choice. It is time to say no to all of the BS that we listen to everyday on the news, with our friends, with our family, with our work colleagues and cultivate a new way of living. kNOw BS. Be bullish about substance because it has power and endurance.

The bull whisperer lives inside you. It has always been there and it always will be.

Set it free.

REFERENCES

Kevin Ashton, "The Creativity of No" (2013), www.medium.com.

Christine Barley, think-differently-about-sheep.com.

Peter Bregman, "18 Minutes: Find Your Focus, Master Distractions," *Business Plus* (2012).

Joseph Campbell, *The Power of Myth* (Turtleback Books, 1991).

Dr. Henry Cloud and Dr. John Townsend, *Boundaries: When to Say Yes, When To Say No* (Zondervan Publishing House, 1992).

Roger Fisher, William Ury, and Bruce Patton, *Getting to Yes: Negotiating Agreement without Giving In*, Harvard Negotiating Project (Penguin Books, 1983).

Marija Gimbutus, *The Language of the Goddess* (Harper Collins, 1991).

Malcolm Gladwell, *The Tipping Point* (Little Brown and Company, 2000).

Gods and Monsters.com.

Heidi Grant Halvorson and E. Tory Higgins, "Do You Play to Win—Or to Not Lose?" *Harvard Business Review* (March 2013).

Steve Jobs, Apple Developer's Conference, 1997.

Dr. Sue Johnson, *Hold Me Tight* (Little Brown and Company, 2011).

C.G. Jung, *The Red Book* (W.W. Norton, 2009).

Andrea Kates, *Find Your Next* (McGraw Hill, 2011).

Kerry Kennedy, RFK Center for Justice and Human Rights speech, 2011.

M. Montgomery, *A Cow's Life: The Surprising History of Cattle and How the Black Angus*

Came to be Home on the Range (Walker and Company, 2004).

Edmund Morris, *Theodore Rex* (Harper Collins, 2001).

Debbie Seaman, "It's Not Just Any Bull in a China Shop," *People Magazine* (January 11, 1982).

Jared Shapiro, *Guns, Germs and Steel* (W.W. Norton, 1997).

Whats-Your-Sign.com.

Everything ever written by David Brooks, Tina Brown, and Maureen Dowd.